Selections from the early print-newspapers in colonial Calcutta, India (1780-1820). Trade and Commerce.

FACSIMILE: A CENTER FOR EARLY PRINT AND SOCIETY.

Copyright © 2014 Facsimile: A Center for Early Print and Society.

All rights reserved.

ISBN: 8192875261
ISBN-13: 978-8192875262

CONTENTS

	Acknowledgments	i
1	Introduction: on how to read 200 year old newspapers.	1
2	On Trade	9
3	On Liberty	17
4	On Property	22
5	On Commerce	26
6	On Subscription Goods/ Copartnership	29
7	On Hospitals	38
8	On Corruption and Crime	42
9	On Opium and Salt Trade	52
10	On Slaves and Abolition	57

ACKNOWLEDGMENTS

For all of us at Facsimile, the Center for Early Print and Society, it has been a delightful journey -- reading old newspapers that had been read by Britishers who had lived and worked in India in the early years of colonization (1780-1820).While the world around us changed, we were busy poring over events that had taken place centuries ago and we would have our coffee and vada-sambhar, making sure our hands were clean – and this can be tricky, while we wondered what to make out of wars fought on the Continent and advertisements about banks and opium chests.

1 INTRODUCTION: ON HOW TO READ 200 YEAR OLD NEWSPAPERS.

We read newspapers that had been printed in the early years of British-East India Company, that is between 1780-1820. How do we read these texts that were written centuries ago and make sense of the printed texts? We cannot elide the fact that they were meant to be textually consumed by the Britishers who had arrived in India as part of the package of colonization. The newspapers were examined with a particular perspective, namely, what was the nature of trade and commerce that evolved in colonial Bengal, India? What was carried over from Britain?

Reading primary texts alters how we theorize. The newspapers allow us to peek into this newly emerging world in Bengal and how socio-technological changes were taking place. We seem to think that these changes seamlessly moved into Bengal without any hiccups. We rarely do have access to these primary texts, as they are hidden in archives. What emerges is the human face of the process of British colonization and not an abstract concept of absolute power.

All the newspapers were multilingual. A government circular or an advertisement would often be simultaneously printed in English, Bengali and Persian. Sadly enough, it has not been possible to transcribe this heteroglossic characteristic of the newspapers in this present book.

Selections from the early newspapers in colonial India.

2 ON TRADE

Calcutta Chronicle

Tuesday; August 27th, 1793. Volume VIII.

East India Trade; Liverpool. Nov. 23; 1792.

AT a Public Meeting of the Merchants, Tradesmen, and other Inhabitants, of the Town of Liverpool, called by the Worshipful the Mayor, for the purpose of taking into consideration the measures to be adopted, in order to obtain Participation of the Trade to the Countries beyond the Cape of Good Hope,

The Worshipful the Mayor in the Chair,

Resolved unanimously,

    I.   That the Creator of the Universe, by endowing different portions of the earth with different products, has laid the foundations of Commerce which, having for its object the supply of mutual wants, and the exchange of mutual comforts, may be safely left to the regulations which mutual interest points out, and should, as far as possible, be free from every restraint.

II. That Monopolies are destructive of these principles, because they provide for the interest of the Monopolist only, and enable him to fix, at his own pleasure, both the rate at which he buys from one country, and sells to another and the charge at which he carries the commodities of each.

III. That the history of the East India Company, affords much striking proofs of the consequences of trusting such powers to the discretion of individuals; and the injuries which their monopoly of the trade between Britain and India has produced to both countries, are of the most serious nature.

IV. That the principle to which many of these are to be traced, is the temptation which the possession of this Monopoly has offered to the East India Company, to exchange the characters of Merchants for those of Warriors and Politicians, by which they have assumed the sovereignty of Twenty Million of Men, with whom Traffick was their first, and ought to have been their only object.

V. That to support a dominion by force, which could not otherwise be supported, they have been led to maintain vast and expensive civil and military establishments, the whole charge of which must be finally defrayed by the people of India or Great Britain, and seems a heavy and cruel, as well as useless burden, on the connexion between the two Countries.

VI. That PEACE is the natural, and ought to be the inseparable attendant of Commerce; that the possession of Continental Territories is valuable only as it is productive of commercial intercourse; and that it is probable the opening of the East India Trade will render less frequent those desolating wars which have so often deluged the soil of that unhappy Country with the blood of its inhabitants, whilst they have been equally fatal to this Country, by the sacrifice of thousands of

British subjects, and the expenditure of millions of British treasure.

VII. That the East India Monopoly prevents the free export of our manufactures to one of the largest and richest regions of the World, where there is reason to believe they might, in the course of open Trade, be increased in their most twenty fold and upwards: -- that under the present system, the exports are conducted without a proper attention to the change of circumstances and reasons; and due means are not employed for opening new sources of Traffic on the Eastern coast of Africa, the island of Madagascar, the countries that lie up the Straits of Babelmandal, and on the shores of the Persian Gulf, with many of the vast profusion of Islands that are scattered throughout the Indian Ocean, all within the limits of the Company's Monopoly, and yielding them little or no advantage; but which the unfettered enterprise and skill of individuals might soon explore and render of the utmost importance.

VIII. That this Monopoly cloaks many of the infant Manufacturers of Britain as they arise, from the power it gives of lowering, at pleasure, the rival Manufactures of India in the Home Market; the loss sustained being laid on such articles as are the produce of the soil of India, which habit has rendered necessary amongst us, and which are not to be obtained elsewhere, a power that more than once has destroyed the manufacture of British Porcelain, and that has employed to oppose and bear down the manufacture of Cotton, now risen to such national importance.

IX. That the injuries to Commerce and Navigation have been proportional, as may be clearly inferred. The practise indeed of employing large vessels on overcharged freights, in an open sacrifice of the interest of the Company itself, to the selfish views of individuals, and is an undeniable proof of the entire departure from the principles of fair Traffic, into which this Monopoly has diverged; that all the branches of those most important manufacturers employed in the building and equipment of shipping, are specially injured under the present system, which also obstructs training of mariners, on which our national safety and prosperity so particularly depend.

X. That the progress of time and experience has now essentially removed the grounds on which the exclusive trade to India was originally supported, viz., the danger and expense of so distant a traffic. The free trade and manufactures of Great Britain, have produced such an influx of wealth, and accumulation of capital, that there is no adventure too heavy for private Merchants, or companies of Merchants, to undertake; the genius, industry, and talents of our people are such, that there is no part of the world to which they cannot make a free trade profitable, and that nearly in proportion to its riches and population; and such are the skill and enterprise of our navigators, that there is no shore so dangerous, no region so remote, as to daunt their spirit, or prevent their approach.

XI. That these facts are capable of colateral proof, from the success with which the Merchants of Portugal carried on a trade to India, without any exclusive charter, for a century and upwards; and still more from the success of the Merchants of North America, who now traverse every parts of the Indian and Pacific Oceans, with vessels of no larger a size than those usually employed on the Atlantic, and who with capitals comparatively insignificant, are opening most advantageous channels of traffic, from which the British Merchant, with prior claims, superior skill, and irresistible capital, is by false policy excluded.

XII. That as it is the nature of trade to force its way through less direct channels, when its natural course is obstructed, the products of Britain now begin to be sent to the East Indies in American bottoms, and those of China and the East Indies to be smuggled into Britain and her Colonies, through America and Ostend[sic],to the injury of the British trader and manufacturer, as well as of the British consumer; all of whose interests are thus palpably sacrificed.

XIII. That these facts, while they point out the impolicy of the present system of the East India Monopoly, demonstrate also the impossibility of its being continued without measures of rigour that the occasion will not justify, and more and more violence against the true principles of commerce now so well understood, and operating with such great and rapid influence on the national prosperity.

XIV. That clear as we are in all these views, we are yet aware that difficulties may attend the overthrow of a false system that has continued so long, and connected itself so widely; and we should condemn all attempts for this purpose, that would sacrifice the interests of those immediately concerned in expiation of the mistaken policy of the nation; but we with the public at large to see the evil of this Monopoly in its full extent, and the collected wisdom of the Legislature to be employed in removing it by methods consistent with true policy and the principles of justice.

XV. That a Petition be therefore presented to Parliament, praying that the whole of this important subject may be taken into consideration, and that we may be permitted to be heard by Council; and, if need be, to adduce evidence in support of our allegations against the renewal of an exclusive Charter, by which our interests, in common with the whole commercial, manufacturing, and by consequence, landed interests of the kingdom are to manifestly injured.

XVI. That a Committee be now appointed to prepare such Petition for the consideration of a Public Meeting, to be hereafter called.

XVII. That the said Committee be requested to correspond with such other towns and places as they may think proper, in order to obtain their co-operation with us on this important business.

XVIII. That these Resolutions be published in such of the London and Country Newspapers, as the said Committee may direct.

Selections from the early newspapers in colonial India.

Calcutta Chronicle

Vol. VII. Tuesday. March 13; 1792.

TO THE EDITOR OF THE CHRONICLE.

Sir,

Deeming the contents of the accompanying paper of some consequences to this country, I have taken to trouble to translate it, ... if you are of the same opinion, you will naturally lay it before your readers. The Author of it was well known here. The millions he speaks of are French lives, values about ten pence each.

I am, Sir,

Yours. Etc..

So well convinced am I, that the trade of the East India Indies conduced on proper principles, ought to be one of the grand branches of our national industry – that I feel it a duty to reply to the objections which have been made against it. It is with regret I observe that the evacuation of Pondicherry, has so far dismissed our expeditions to India that it may be said the trade is almost annihilated.

...

Our establishments in India, have been represented as a point in the universe, and which could form no other object than the support of a commerce, luxurious in itself, and destructive of our manufactures.

...

It was not formerly perceived that the trade to India was detrimental to circulation; and unless very severe prohibitory laws are made – and which could never be applicable to bullion or bills drawn from India

– we must constantly be tributary to England or Holland, for the productions of Asia, which would sink that balance whose equilibrium we seek to establish.

The great power of the English in India, their vast possessions and the importance of their revenues, shall be put in contrast with our pitiful establishments....

But should any event they say, cause a rupture with England – What resources can, we have in a country where the English are everything – and we are nothing. Where they, with their own revenues, can furnish their expenses, whilst we cannot succeed in our's without succour from Europe?

...

The last war in India, cost us about two hundred millions. The following is what it cost the English:

...

Thus, gentlemen, there are twelve hundred millions, concerned in India, without reckoning the profits which the Company have made in their trade.

200

3 ON LIBERTY

Calcutta Chronicle

Tuesday. November 6, 1792. Number 355. Volume vii.

Translation of the Letter Written by M. De La Fayette, to the French King. When he sent him a copy of his letter to the National Assembly.

From the entrenched Camp of Maubeuge, the 16th of June, 1792.

The fourth year of liberty.

Sire,

I have the honour to forward to your Majesty, a copy of my letter to the National Assembly, wherein your Majesty will recognize the sentiments which have always animated my life. Your Majesty knows with what ardour, with what confidence, I have devoted myself to the cause of liberty, the sacred principles of humanity, of equality, and of justice: that I have always been the adversary of factions, the enemy of licentiousness, and that I never acknowledged any authority which

I thought illegitimate: your Majesty knows my devotion to your Constitutional authority, and my attachment to your person. These, Sire, form the basis of my letter to the National Assembly; …

Continue strong, Sire, in that authority which the National Assembly has delegated to you, in the generous resolution of defending the principles of the Constitution against all its enemies; and may this resolution, supported by all the acts of your private life, as well as a firm and complete exercise of the Royal Power, become the pledge of that harmony, which, at this critical moment, cannot fail to be established between the Representatives, elected by the people and their hereditary representation. It is in this resolution, Sire, that of your and the country's welfare consists. In this you will find the friends of liberty and all good Frenchmen, ranged around your throne to defend it against the plots of the rebels, and the enterprises of the factious.

…

(Signed) LA FAYETTE

TRANSLATION

OF A LETTER FROM M. LA FAYETTE TO THE

NATIONAL ASSEMBLY, READ IN THE SETTING.

ON MONDAY, THE EIGHTEENTH OF JUNE.

From the entrenched Camp of Mauberge, 16th June, 1792.

THE FOURTH YEAR OF LIBERTY.

GENTLEMEN,

At the moment (too long deferred perhaps) in which I was about to call your attention to the great interest of the public, and point out among our dangers, the conduct of a Minister, whom I long ago accused in my correspondence; I find that he is now unmasked, and has sunk under his own intrigues; … The fate of France rests principally upon its representatives; the Nation expects its welfare from them; but in giving themselves a constitution, the mode by which it can be preserved is clearly prescribed.

Persuaded as I am, Gentlemen, that, as the Rights of Man are the law of all Constituent Assemblies, Constitution becomes the law of those very legislators, who have formed it: it is therefore, yourselves to whom I ought to denounce the too powerful efforts, which are made to divert you from those rules, which you have promised to follow.

…

You ought, Gentlemen, to curb them [the enemies of France]; but you will only have the power, so long as you are Constitutional and Just.

Certainly you will repress then, but see first, what passes within your own bosoms, and around you.

And, shall I then longer delay to fulfil this duty, whilst every day weakens the constitutional authority, substitutes party spirit for the will of the people, whilst the audacity of these agitators impose silence on the peaceful citizen, drive away useful men, and whilst the devotion these sectaries bear towards each other, holds the place of public and private virtue, which in a free country ought to be the austere, and the only means of obtaining the first places of Government?

…

As for me, Gentlemen, who espoused the American cause, as the instant that her ambassadors declared to me that all was lost; who have henceforward vowed persevering defence of the liberty and sovereignty of the people; who, on the 11th of July, 1789, in presenting to my country a declaration of rights, dared say to her — *For a nation to be free, it is sufficient that she wills it.* I appear before you, full of confidence in the justice of our cause, of contempt for the cowards who defeat it, of contempt for the traitors who would ruin it. I declare, that unless the French nation is the most vile in the universe, she can, and ought to resist the combinations of the kings who have coalesced against her. It is not, certainly, in the midst of my brave army, that timid sentiments are permitted: patriotism, energy, discipline, patience, mutual confidence, all the civil and military virtues I find here.

Here the principles of liberty and equality are cherished; the laws respected; property sacred: here are known neither calumny or faction; and when I reflect that France has several millions of men who may become soldiers, I ask myself, to what degree of baseness would an immense people, still stronger by their natural resources, than the defence of art, be reduced, in opposing to an enormous confederacy, the advantages of a perfect union? That the cowardly idea of sacrificing of sacrificing her sovereign, of bartering her liberty, and putting in treaty her declaration of rights should appear one of the possibilities of that futurity which is advancing so rapidly upon us!

...

In short, that the reign of CLUBS, annihilated by you, give place to the Law; their usurpations, to the firm and independent exercise of the Constitutional Authority, their disorganised maxims, to the true principles of Liberty; their delirious fury, to the calm and constant courage of a nation, who know their rights, and to defend them in short, their sectary combinations, to the true interests of the country; which should unite all those, to whom her abasement and ruin are not objects of atrocious rejoicing, and infamous speculation.

Such, gentlemen, are the sentiments which are submitted to the National Assembly, as they have been submitted to the King, by a

Citizen; to whom no one certainly will dispute the love of liberty, of whom different factions would hate less, had he not raised himself above them by disinterestedness; to whom silence would be more becoming, if, like many others, he had been indifferent to the glory of the National Assembly; ...

(*Signed*) LA FAYETTE

4 ON PROPERTY

BENGAL HERALD

CALCUTTA. SATURDAY. JUNE 13, 1829.

ON THE PROSPERITY OF BENGAL IN 1829.

The value of land may be assigned as the more immediate and the lesser restrictions on commerce and greater introduction of Europeans, as the primary cause of this beneficial change. Many facts may be brought forward to strengthen each of these assertions, and, as they speak for themselves, need no preface. Land has been purchased in Calcutta thirty years ago for fifteen rupees, not it is worth and would sell for three hundred Rupees!!! Many similar examples might be adduced. By means of this territorial value, a class of society has sprung into existence, that were before unknown; these are placed between the aristocracy and the poor, and are daily forming, a most influential class. Previous to their formation, the wealth of the country was in the hands of a few individuals, while all others were dependent on them, and the bulk of the people were in a state of abject poverty of mind and body, which will perhaps form a juster reason for the pervading moral bondage of the Hindoos, than the more specious ones of climate or religion.

The advantages to be derived from this change are incalculable, not merely as regards the Hindoos themselves, but as affecting the prosperity and stability of the British Indian Empire. It is the dawn of a new era. Whenever such an order of men have been created, freedom has its train. Do we need an example? – look at England after the Norman conquest, when the people were Serfs, and the landlords lived as the Zemindars of this country did some years ago; but watch their progress up to the eighth Henry when wealth became more equally diffused, and continue the view until the son of a butcher dethroned and decapitated a monarch, and made the Republic of England feared and admired by the world. Do we need an instance of the misfortunes of having only two ranks in a country; look at Spain, where every man that can afford it, lives without either mental or bodily labour, and claims the rank of a Hidalgo. Need we go farther – look at unhappy Poland, where the peasantry are sold with the soil. With the many examples of this nature before us, it may not be deemed presumptuous to assert, that this middling class of inhabitants in Bengal, afford the most cheering indications of any exist at the present period.

Among the beneficial effects already derived from this new order of things, is the greater circulation of money – this admits of proof. In the first place, the cowries are nearly extinct in Calcutta, and in the course of few years they will scarcely be seen in Bengal. Ten years ago, a labourer in Calcutta received two rupees a month – now he is not satisfied with less than four or five, and there is even a scarcity of workmen. A cabinet-maker formerly received eight rupees a month – now he obtains sixteen or twenty rupees for the same period. The price of labour is also increased in the country. Twelve field labourers were formerly to be had for one rupee a day – now six men can only be had for a similar sum. Land for paddy was used to be rented for one rupee a beegah now a Zemindar asks from his tenants, three or four rupees a beegah. The rich which was wont to be sold for eight annas a maund, may now be averaged at two rupees a maund; and the entire district of a Zemindary is now cultivated, when formerly not one half was used; this is in consequence of the Indigo planting.

Let us now proceed to investigate the causes of this change. We think it may be demonstrated that the throwing open of the trade, and the admission of Europeans, even with all the restrictions that have been imposed, are the leading causes: because, previous to the charter of 1813, the state of the country did not bear those decided marks of improvement which it has done since. A baneful monopoly checked the exertions of individuals, and, by its magnitude, deterred many from embarking in speculations which have since proved profitable pursuits. The arrival of European settlers has encouraged the manufacture of Indigo, which, while it benefitted themselves, enriched both England and India, and developed, in some degree, the capabilities of both soil and climate of the latter.

Those who have called out so loudly against the increased facility for our trade with Liverpool, Glasgow, &c., have adduced, as an argument in their favour, that the India market has become glutted with English manufactures, and that those who have been exported them have suffered severely. This event happens in all similar changes, and is productive of the most beneficial effects. The cheapness of the article induces purchasers, and a taste, before unknown, is thereby created, which, on the goods attaining their standard value, will, if possible, continue to be gratified; hence new importations are encouraged, and the happiness of the provider and consumer increased. It is, however, evident, that on such an occurrence a reciprocity of trade must take place, and that if England expects that India will prove a large mart for her produce, she must remove the restrictive, almost prohibitory duties on Asiatic produce, which are disgraceful to a free country. The East India Company alone, it is said, draw annually from India *four Millions sterling in bullion – upwards of two millions* of which are for the payment of dividends to the share-holders, and the remainder for the expenses of the home establishment.

We have conversed with many Native gentlemen who, themselves, are astonished at the increased value of their property, and when asked to assign a cause, they attribute it to the importation of European produce, skill and energy.

If such effects have been already produced, what may not be expected by the equalization of duties on East and West India Sugars – the importation of Machinery – and the introduction and settlement of Europeans, freed from the odious, overbearing threat of deportation, so repugnant, so palling to the feelings of every man possessed of a spark of liberty.

5 ON COMMERCE

Calcutta Chronicle

Volume III. Tuesday. April 10, 1792. Number 325.

[A LETTER ON TRADE]

Bengal ought not to depend on the sales in Leaden-hall street: to reduce such a kingdom to such dependence would be the highest indiscretion. Great Britain should, and does wish to, draw from their estate in Asia, what the estate in Asia can afford to pay, and not a farthing more.

…

I look up to Sir William Jones as to the first linguist in the world; I suppose he must have read the History of all the Nations of the earth, and have and do now exist – to him I appeal, whether the division of property in all free states is not the life and soul of liberty. India owes to Europe a vast balance: the Portuguese forced back a part, and planted a motley religion, ignorance and superstition, in the place of it: the policy of the Dutch was but little better. I hope the

English will not kill the bird for the golden egg.

...

An indifferent onlooker.

CALCUTTA GAZETTE

Calcutta, February 21, 1788.

General Bank of India

NOTICE IS HEREBY GIVEN,

THAT a GENERAL QUARTERLY MEETING of the PROPIETOR'S will be held at the BANK on MONDAY the 3rd March, at 9 o' clock in the forenoon, at which time two DIRECTORS are to Elected in the room of W. COWPER, and W. BARTON, Esqrs. Resigned.

By order of the Directors,

T. GOWAN, Sec.

Facsimile: A center for early print and society.

CALCUTTA GAZETTE

Calcutta, February 21, 1788.

GEORGE ROACH AND HENRY JOHNSTON,

late of Calcutta, Merchants, take the liberty of informing those Gentlemen in India who may have business at Lisbon that requires an Agent, that they have opened a House there under the firm of GEORGE ROACH & Co. for transacting Commission Business of all kinds. The greatest attention will be paid by Mr. ROACH who is settled at Lisbon, to all Orders, Commissions, &c. &c. that the House may be favoured with from Gentlemen in India; and HENRY JOHNSTON (at the India Agency Office, Old Bond Street) will execute with fidelity any Orders or Commission Business in London.

Bengal Herald

Calcutta, Saturday. June 13. 1829.

NEW BANK

We beg to call the attention of the Public to the Meeting which is to be held on Monday next, at the Exchange Rooms, by the shareholders of the "New General Bank." – A book lies open for the signature of such as propose investing their property in this Establishment. Of its utility, nay of its absolute necessity, there can scarcely be a difference of opinion. For instance, suppose that the Charter of the E. I. Company should not be renewed in three years, the people of England could not take on themselves the payment of the Company debts, and the only alternative would be to declare the Honourable East India Company bankrupt, …

6 ON SUBSCRIPTION GOODS/ COPARTNERSHIP

Supplement To The Calcutta Gazette.

THURSDAY. JANUARY. 6. 1791.

VOL. XIV. # 358.

FORT WILLIAM, December 31, 1790.

Public notice is hereby given, that Subscription will be received, on or before the 31st of January, 1791, for raising a Fund to be applied to the provision of an Investment for Europe in 1791, for the benefit of the Subscribers, in the manner following, wiz.

1st. The Amount subscribed is to form one common Stock, in which each person shall have an interest proportionate to his Subscription.

2nd. The sum subscribed is to be paid into the General Treasury in the following proportions:

¼ on or before the 15th February 1791.

¼ - 1st April.

¼ - 1st June.

¼ - 1st August.

3d. Persons failing in the due payment of their Instalment shall be considered as having forfeited their right to any benefit from the Investment. And the money they may have paid shall be returned to them at the end of twelve months from the time of payment, with Interest at the rate of Eight per Cent. per Annum.

4th. The amount subscribed shall be invested in Piece Goods, under the direction of the Board of Trade, and through the Agency of the Company's Servants under their authority, in the same manner as if a like amount were invested upon account of the Company, in addition to the Investment which the Governor General in Council has resolved to provide for the year 1791.

5th. The Board of Trade, in arranging all, or any, of the orders to the Factories undermentioned for the Subscription Goods, will exercise their judgment, as they do with respect to the Company's Investment, with this exception, that they will not order any assortments, which, by the accounts received in the course of the last season, did not yield a profit to the Company

Benaras	Gollagore	Malda	Santipore
Chittagong	Hurriaul	Midnapore	Soonamookey
Commercolly	Hurripaul	Patna	
Cossimbazar	Keerpoy	Radnagore	
Dacca	Luckipore	Rungpore	

6th. The Subscription Goods shall be provided at the Factories in the mats with the Company's Goods, without any discrimination of property and shall be examined at the Export Ware House, and reported upon as though the whole were the Company's.

7th. In the course of the shipping season of 1791-2, that is to say, between the 1st October 1791 (or earlier should circumstances admit) and the 15th March 1792, a separation shall be made of the Goods ordered for the Subscription from the Company's Goods; and, in making the separation, care will be taken to make the proportion of quality in each assortment for the Company, and for the Subscribers, as nearly equal as the circumstances of the business will admit of.

8th. The Subscription Goods shall be sent to England upon the Company's ships of next season, and sold at the Company's sales on account of the Subscribers.

9th. They will be distributed upon the Company's ships according to circumstances in respect to Tonnage and Value, and it will be endeavored to divide the Silk upon two or more ships of the season, according to the amount that may be subscribed and the times of the ships failing. In order to afford the Subscribers an opportunity of making Insurances in Europe, none of their Goods will be put on the two first ships.

10th. After the separation of the Goods in the Export Ware house, the silk of Fire, Rivers, and Seas shall be upon the Subscribers.

11th. The value of the Subscription Goods will be ascertained from the Factory Invoices, to which value shall be added their proportion of Charges embaling and Merchandize on the Invoice, the agents Commission as paid by the Company, and an advance of Sixteen per Cent, computed upon the value exclusive of Commission and Charges.

12th. The Charges of Shipping the Subscription Goods, and of Embaling in Calcutta such as come down from the factories, not properly embaled for Europe, will be charged to the Subscribers.

13th. Freight will be charged upon the Goods at the Company's Charter-party rate of the ensuing season; with an advance of Twenty per Cent. thereupon, as an equivalent for Kentledge and Demurrage.

14th. The Goods will be subjected in England to the usual charge upon private trade, Five per Cent. Company's Duties, and Two per Cent. for Warehouse-room. The National Duties and Charges will, of course, be borne by the Subscribers.

15th. The Governor General in Council will recommend to the Court of Directors that, the Subscription Goods be sold at the same time with the Company's Goods, laden on the same ship; and that, in case only part of a Cargo be sold at one time, the sale of the Subscription Goods of that Cargo, be in just proportion to the sale of the Company's Goods.

16th. The net proceeds shall be divided among the Subscribers according to their respective Subscription; and the Governor General in Council will recommend to the Court of Directors that, immediately on the realization of the proceeds of each Cargo, dividends shall be paid to the Subscribers.

17th. Each Subscriber, on completing the payment of his Subscription, will forthwith be furnished with a Certificate, in triplicate, entitling him, or his order, to his Share of the produce of the Goods to be sent to Europe.

18th. No Subscription, less than Current Rupees 5000, will be received.

19th. The Governor General in Council holds himself at liberty to relinquish the Plan altogether in the event of the amount tendered not being in his judgment, of a magnitude worthy of attention.

20th. Persons desirous of subscribing will be pleased to notify their intentions, and the sum they mean to subscribe, to the Secretary of the Board of Trade.

Selections from the early newspapers in colonial India.

Published by Order of the Governor General in Council.

B. HAY, *Secretary to the Government.*

ADDITIONAL SUPPLEMENT

TO THE

CALCUTTA GAZETTE.

VOL. XV.   THURSDAY, March 3, 1791.

No. 366

GANGES ASSURANCE COMPANY (with the Sanction of Government) for the BENEFIT of the INTERNAL TRADE.

Whereas, the INTERNAL TRADE of INDIA, is liable to much inconvenience, loss, and delay from the want of an OFFICE of ASSURANCE, to assure the BOATS, GOODS, and MERCHANDIZE of TRADERS and others; the Business being almost entirely in the Hands of the NATIVE BANKERS, who are guided solely by Caprice and Custom, without any knowledge of true principles of assuring as practiced in European Governments; and as in particular, a Custom prevails which is the source of continual Suits in the Supreme Court and Courts of Adawlut, viz. "That Goods sunk and recovered, however damaged, absolve the Insurer," and as much delay is also occasioned by their requiring a previous proof of Interest before they will under write at all; besides, the great difficulty which attends adjusting and recovering losses when they do happen; it has therefore, and for Sundry other good causes and considerations been proposed, to erect, and establish, and there is erected and established at Mirzapoor in the Zemindary of Benaras, (the sanction of Government having been first had and obtained) a HOUSE of ASSURANCE, or INSURANCE, under the Firm of the GANGES ASSURANCE COMPANY; upon a liberal Plan of Reciprocal Benefit, with a view to remedy the loss, inconvenience, and delays complained of. And in order to render the present establishment of every possible use to the Internal Trade Agents will be appointed at the several stations of Calcutta, Dacca, Patna, Moorshedabad and Chittagong, as well as in such other Station or Stations, as may hereafter be deemed advisable, with powers to grant Policies, and otherwise transact the business of the Company, as if the same was actually under the inspection of the Managers at Mirzapoor. For the further information of the Public, the first, 5th and 9th Clauses of the Deed of Copartnership with the 14th, 15th, 16th, 17th, 19th, 20th, 21st and 22nd Articles of the Laws and Regulations for the Interior Management of the Company are here subjoined:

CLAUSES of the DEEDS of COPARTNERSHIP.

FIRST.

That the said Parties of these Presents, their Executors, Administrators and Assigns shall, be remain and continue a Society or Copartnership, for the Assurance or Insurance, on all property sent down or up the Ganges, down or up any Rivers, Channel or Channels communicating with the Ganges, usually known by the term of the Internal Navigation: as also on all property conveyed by Land or by Water, to, or through any of the interior parts of India, for any time not exceeding the period of the Copartnership from the day of the date hereof, for and during, and unto the full end and term of Five Years, now next ensuing, and fully to be completed and ended; if they the said Parties, or any three of them, shall so long live;

and that the Business thereof, shall be managed and carried on, at Mirzapoor aforesaid at or in such House or Houses, Place or Places, as the said Parties, or Copartners present, shall from time to time think fit; and that the said Society shall be distinguished, and called, by the name of the GANGES ASSURANCE COMPANY, or shall bear such other Name, Stile, or Title, from time to time, as the said Copartners or the Major part of them, for the time being, shall think fit.

FIFTH

That all Losses will shall or may happen during this Copartnership, shall be adjusted, and paid in manner following (that is to say) all Losses which shall happen within the Province of Behar, and District of Zemindary of Benaras, within Two Months, to be computed from the day of its Notification to the Acting Managers at Mirzapoor. All Losses which shall happen within the Province of Bengal, (the district of Chittagong excepted) within Three Months, to be computed as aforesaid; and all Losses which shall happen within the district of Chittagong, or in any other Place or Places in the interior parts of India (the course of the Ganges and its communications as aforesaid excepted,) within Four Months to be computed from the time of its notification at Mirzapoor.

NINTH

That Agents be appointed, on behalf of the Society, at Calcutta, Dacca, Patna, Moorshedabad and Chittagong, or elsewhere, as it shall be deemed expedient for the advantage of the Society; which Agents shall be authorized, and empowered, to grant any Policy or Policies, Instrument or Instruments, to make Assurance or Insurance, on account of the said Copartnership; and every policy or Policies, Instrument or Instruments for the Insurance of any Boat or Vessel, Goods or Merchandise, which shall be made by such Agent or

Agents consormably to the authority which shall or may be given them, shall be at all times, binding upon the whole of the said Copartners, their Executors, Administration or Assigns, in the same manner, as if the same had been signed by the Committee in the manner before-mentioned.

ARTICLES in the LAWS and REGULATIONS.

FOURTEENTH

That the Acting Managers, the Agent or Agents at each, or all the Stations as aforesaid, shall, and may Assure or Insure on account of the Company, agreeable to the 9th and 11th Articles of the Deed Copartnership, any Boat, Boats or Vessel, Goods or Merchandise, laden or to be laden, upon any Boat, Boats or Vessel provided always, that the value laden or to laden, on any One Boat or Vessel as, aforesaid, shall not exceed Sicca Rupees ………. without any previous proof of Interest; the same having hitherto been required by the Native Assurers, and the causes of much inconvenience and delay to the Internal Trade.

FIFTEENTH

All Loss or Losses, Damage or Damages, which shall or may happen, to, in, or upon any Boat, Boats or Vessel, Goods or Merchandise, laden or to be laden on any Boat, Boats or Vessel assured by the Company, where the same shall be under Five per Cent of the whole value at risk, such Loss or losses as aforesaid to be borne by the assured.

SIXTEENTH

All Loss or Losses, Damage or Damages, which shall or may happen to, in, or upon any Boat, Boats or Vessel, Goods or Merchandize, laden or to be laden, in, or upon, any Boat, Boats or Vessel, assured by the Company, when the same shall be above Five, but under Ten per Cent, of the whole value at Risk, the said Loss or Losses, Damage or Damages, to be borne by the assured; but such a proportion of the Premium shall be returned as if the assured had himself stood to Ten per Cent, of the whole risk.

SEVENTEENTH

All Loss or Losses, Damage or Damages, which shall or may happen to, in, or upon any Boat, Boats or Vessel, Goods or Merchandize, laden or to be laden, on any Boat, Boats or Vessel, assured by the Company, when the same shall exceed Ten per Cent, of the whole value so at Risk, the same shall be adjusted by Average, as is customary in like cases; or the assured may abandon the whole at risk to the Company as he shall judge most to his advantage.

...

The business will commence at Mirzapoor, and at each of the aforementioned Stations, on the 20th March ensuing. The Rates of Assurance (which are to be on time) with the names of the Agent or Agents at the several Stations as above, will be published in a subsequent Gazette.

Mirzapoor, Feb. 19. 1791.   Acting Managers { FRANCIS LAWRENCE

{WILLIAM CULLEN

7 ON HOSPITALS

CALCUTTA GAZETTE

HOSPITAL.

Calcutta, September 27th, 1792.

Agreeably to the Advertisements published in the Gazette on the 20th and 27th instant, requesting the attendance of such persons as were disposed to support the plan, heretofore proposed for establishing an hospital for the relief of Natives, requiring the assistance of a Surgeon; a meeting of the principal Inhabitants of Calcutta, was this day held for the purpose of carrying the proposed institution into effect; when the following resolutions were agreed to.

RESOLVED, that an Hospital be established for the relief of Natives, requiring the professional assistance of a Surgeon.

RESOLVED, that the Management of the Hospital be vested in an equal number of European and Native Governors, being Inhabitants of Calcutta.

RESOLVED, that a Committee be appointed to procure and receive subscriptions for the support of the institution and to prepare a plan for the management thereof.

RESOLVED, that the Committee consists of the following Gentlemen:

Mr. SPEKE

COWPER

The Reverend Mr. OWEN

Mr. VANDERHEYDEN

DICK,

MEYER,

COLEBROOK,

LAMBERT,

FLEMING,

WILSON,

DOWDESWELL,

MORRIS, and

BARRETTO.

AGREED, that the committee be requested to call a general meeting of the Subscribers as soon as the plan or Institution shall have been prepared for their consideration. The Committee having met pursuant to the above resolutions and taken such measures for giving effect to the plan proposed, as the shortness of the time has hitherto admitted oft; have the satisfaction to inform the public, that Government have been pleased to signify their intention, that Surgeons shall be appointed from among the Company's Servants to do duty at the Hospital, which it has been resolved to establish.

Subscriptions shall be received either by a donation to the fund for the support of the Institution, or by monthly payments at the following places:

THE HINDUSTAN BANK,

FAIRLIE, REID and Co.

BURGH AND BARBER

LAMBERT, ROSS, and Co.

COCEKERELL, TRAIL and CO.

HAMILTON and ABERDEIN

COLVINS and BAZETT

PERREAU and PALLING

J. and L. BARRETTO

UDNEY, FRUSHDAN, & LAPRIMADAY

GEORGE AND THOMAS GOWAS.

The following is a List of Subscribers.

	Sa Rs.
Cornwallis, --	3,000
P. Speke, --	1,500
Robert Wilson, --	1,000
J. Buller, --	500

Selections from the early newspapers in colonial India.

D. Vanderheyen, --	500
Charles Chapman, --	300
John Eliot, --	200
G. Dowdeswell, --	500
G.C. Meyer, --	500
A. Lambert, --	500
C. Shakespeare, --	100
J. Owen, --	600
William Dick, --	300
Lula Barretto, --	500
John Fleming, --	500
Edmund Morris, --	

8 ON CORRUPTION AND CRIME

THE CALCUTTA GAZETTE

OR

ORIENTAL ADVERTISER

PUBLISHED BY AUTHORITY AND POSTAGE FREE

VOL. VIII.   THURSDAY, September 13, 1787.
[No. 185]

HOUSE OF COMMONS.

MONDAY, APRIL 2.

CHARGE AGAINST Mr. HASTINGS.

The order of the day being read for going into a Committee on the charges of Mr. Hastings.

Mr. Sheridan rose and in a speech which took nearly two hours and a quarter in the delivery, reviewed and enforced, with his usual perspicuity and elegance, the whole of the charge which was founded on the illegal acceptance of Presents by Mr. Hastings. Favoured as he had been, he said, by the indulgent attention of the Committee on a late occasion, ... the propriety of the present accusation, he could not refuse his aid to those who with equal zeal in the cause, had their attention divided by more varied occupations. The subject which he had to produce, was in itself cold and dry. ... It appeared to him on the contrary, that nothing could be more uniform than the corruption of Mr. Hastings. He was everything else by fits and starts, but he was corrupt by system and by method. His cruelty approached its object in a violent gust, but happily in general of short duration – his resentments were a storm tornado – but his corruption was as the Monsoon, which constantly blew from the same point, without abating of its force, or varying in its direction.

...

The first circumstance of this nature which he thought it necessary to notice, was the bribe of two lakhs of rupees received from Cheyt Singh, the unfortunate Rajah of Benaras, on the 21st of June, 1780. The first mention of this affair, which tended to excite suspicion was made in a letter from Hastings on the 20th of November following, in which he expressed himself as follows: "My present relation for reverting to this conduct, is to obviate the false conclusion or purposed misrepresentations which may be made of it; either as an artifice of ostentation, or the effect of corrupt influence, by assuring you that the money by whatever means it came into my possession, was not my own; that I had myself no right to it, nor would nor could have received it, but for the occasion which prompted me to avail myself of the accidental means which were at that instant offered me of accepting, and converting it to the use of the Company." – The purpose here alluded to was a particular operation of the Mahratta war, on the propriety of which the members of the Council had disagreed with the Governor General. But though two letters had been afterwards written by Mr. Hastings, in which this circumstance was mentioned, the Directors were still in total ignorance of the person from whom this has been received until it was after a long interval discovered by Major Scott, on this examination before the Select Committee in 1782, who believed it probable that the Rajah had chosen rather to make a free gift of that sum to the Governor General than to lend it to the Company at an interest of eight percent, thinking that a protection would be secured thereby, which Mr. Hastings had certainly never held out: such, added the Major, where the prejudices of the people; -- such he should rather there have said was the corruption of the Government, and such the usage which compelled the natives of India to purchase that protection which they had a right to demand.

There was in this transaction one circumstance which was highly worthy of observation. On the 21st of June this money had been received, by which the Rajah had imagined that he should purchase an amnesty for the past and a safety for the future; and on the 22nd of the same month, on the very day following, appeared on the council book the first hostile minute of the Governor-General, complaining in the strongest language of the contumacy and insolence of the Rajah – Cheyt Singh had all along pleaded poverty, as an excuse for his noncompliance with the demands made on him. Mr. Hastings had undoubtedly not increased his ability to discharge these demands by accepting two lakhs privately, when the withholding of four lakhs, was the object of public contest. Here was a contradiction which Mr. Hastings alone could explain, or a cruelty which it seemed reserved for him to inflict. The most obvious construction of the business, in its present shape was, that Mr. Hastings imagined, that the person who was so easily made a dupe to private extortion, was of course the most eligible object for public plunder. The circumstances as related in his defence, threw not the smallest light on the mysterious parts of this transaction. He there seemed to content himself with saying, that the object for which the money was received, being defeated, it was beneath him to return it: it was therefore deposited in the Treasury of Calcutta, not in the name of the Company, but that of Mr. Hastings; and the principal result of the transaction seemed to be, that it had so far ripened the experience of the Governor General, that he never afterwards discovered a transaction of a similar nature until active investigation trod so close at his heels, that he despaired of concealment, and caught therefore at the seeming merit of discovery.

...

He had mentioned, that his principal inducement to accept the present, was for the purpose of discharging the arrears due to the troops, by whom he was then accompanied; for this purpose those bills could by no means answer, as the individual credit of Mr. Hastings, on his arrival at Benaras would be definitely superior to the credit, either of the distressed Nabob, or of Gopal Das, on whom the bills were drawn; -- again it was pretended, to give some plausibility to the motives of the donation, that one part of it had been given to Mrs. Hastings. He should be sorry to introduce a Lady's name on the occasion, if it was not for the purpose of exculpating her from any share in the transaction; for it appeared in the evidence of Mr. Middleton, who was then on the spot, that Mrs. Hastings, to whom it had been stated that one half of this present had been personally given, did not arrive until the money had been received, and the business entirely concluded. This bribe therefore had been unfortunate in every respect.

[ON THE JUDICIARY]

CALCUTTA COURIER

Saturday, April 14th, 1832.

At the Meeting which took place this day at the Town Hall, pursuant to notice by the Sheriff, we found ourselves in a crowd of many hundred persons, pretty composed of Europeans, East Indians, and Natives. The Chair was taken by Mr. Hare, a little after eleven, and

Mr. Clarke opened the business with a good speech explanatory of the object of the meeting. He cited an opinion, expressed on the bench by Sir Edward Ryan, in favour of an extension of the Jury System, and concluded by moving a Resolution to the effect, that, in the opinion of the meeting, the introduction of Trial by Jury in the Supreme Court, in Civil cases, would be advantageous to the interests of society.

The Resolution was attended by Mr. Wynch in a speech of some length, remarkably well delivered and teaming with eloquent passages. He was glad to see so much public spirit exhibited in Calcutta, and that public meetings were not confined to gratulatory addresses. He was proud to find himself associated in such a cause with members of the legal profession. We ought all to be acquainted with the laws of the country (here he quoted Blackstone) – he had seen several men of higher standing than himself arraigned before the Supreme Court; would any of them, would the public, have been satisfied with any other trial than that of a Jury? The Immortal Exile of St. Helena had introduced the system into his Code. It was above half a century since the question was first agitated here. Mr. Wynch then read a petition of the 1st June, 1761, in which grief and surprise were expressed, that Juries in Civil cases were not permitted in Calcutta. He referred also to some passages of the *Calcutta Journal*, written in 1821 – and to a petition of 1770, praying for the extension of Trial by Jury in Civil cases. He would not conclude without expressing his hope, humble disciple as he was of the great Jurist Bentham, that Oaths would be dispensed with – "Swear not at all," said the Gospel. He was persuaded that the imposition of Oaths, being opposed to Native prejudices, would be a serious bar to the effective working of a system which it was the merit of the Supreme Court to introduce into this country.

Mr. Cochrane rose to oppose the motion. He differed entirely from his learned friend the mover of the Resolution, both as to the necessity of the measure and all its details. (We cannot give even the heads of Mr. Cochrane's impassioned speech, which excited a good deal of attention and surprise, and some amusement. His main objection seemed to be, that Natives were so given to perjury that they could not be trusted as Jurymen.)

Mr. Turton followed in reply, and during a quarter of an hour kept the meeting in a roar of laughter.

He defended the zeal of his friend Mr. Wynch and the other "conspirators," who had been so pointedly alluded to by the last speaker, and illustrated his argument with several happy allusions. It was something new to hear admiration of the Judges from Mr. Cochrane; but he particularly admired his friend's invocation to the rising sun, the new Chief Justice. Mr. Cochrane had expressed dissatisfaction at the verdicts in criminal cases. He (Mr. Turton) was more displeased with the decisions in civil cases. The Judges might be good judges of law, but could not be good judges of fact in this Country. Juries had existed a thousand years in England; they were lately established in Scotland, and were spreading over Europe. He was satisfied they would be highly beneficial here.

Baboo Dwarkanath Tagore said a few words, chiefly justifying the interest taken by the Natives in these meetings, in answer to remarks in a letter signed "Jackall" which had appeared in the *Calcutta Courier*. He concluded by moving, that Juries, in Civil cases, should be granted at the option of either Plaintiff or Defendant.

Mr. C. Prinsep was glad to see (he might fairly say so,) the unanimity which prevailed. He was not discouraged by the ill success of the petition of 1799, at a time when it was so difficult to muster even a Grand Jury, that the Military volunteered their services to make a respectable show. The Natives then took no interest in the question. Things were now vastly changed. As to the antiquity of our Jury system, he believed the Punchayet to be still more ancient. Mr. Princep concluded by moving, that the following Gentlemen form a Committee to prepare the intended Petition to Parliament, viz. Sir

John Grant, Colonel Young, Mr. Gordon, Mr. Turton, Mr. Hare, Mr. L. Clarke, Baboo Dwarkanath Tagore and Baboo Russocomar Tagore.

This resolution was seconded by Baboo Rassomoy Dutt. He cited the opinions of Munro, Malcolm, and a former Judge, in favor of the Punchayet, in a very neat and appropriate speech.

At the suggestion of Mr. Longueville Clarke, the names of Mr. Princep and Mr. Kyd, were added to the Committee.

[ON THE JUDICIAL SYSTEM]

CALCUTTA GAZETTE

June 23, 1818.

SUPREME COURT

MONDAY, JUNE 15, 1818

On this-day commenced the third Session of Oyer and Terminer and General Goal Delivery, for this year. The usual formalities having gone through, the Grand Jury composed of the following Gentlemen were addressed by the Honourable Mr. Justice East.

The usual Proclamation having been made, the Lord Chief Justice delivered a charge to the Grand Jury, in substance as follows:

"Gentlemen of the Grand Jury"

"Considering the interval which has elapsed since the last Sessions, the number of offences stated in the Calendar, does not appear to exceed the usual estimate; and as most of them consist in thefts of different sorts, depending altogether upon the simple facts sworn to by the witnesses, it is not necessary to trouble you with any observation upon such cases, which are familiar to your experience.

"Of those which are marked by any peculiarity or aggravation, one of the most prominent is the case of *Audaree* (alias *Soodo*, alias *Abdaur*) *Neloo*, *Buzoo* and *Shukoor*, against whom with others unknown, the Coroner's Jury have returned an inquisition of murder. The account of the transaction is to be collected shortly from the deposition of an Ayah of the name of *Garcia*, living in the service of William Gorham and his wife."

…

"It is impossible to notice without regret that the present Calendar contains several charges against Chinese Inhabitants of Calcutta; - one of Burglary and Larceny, and two others for desperate assaults and stabbing; in each of which, several persons are concerned: these, and the late records of the Court, bear witness against the growing insubordination and malpractices of the class. It might have been expected, that passing from under the rule of one of the most severe, to one of the mildest governments in the world, the change would have operated more beneficially upon them – than those instances give reason to fear. The late frequent charges against some of them, at the Police, for the nuisance of public, and often of fraudulent gaming; for thieving, violence, and even for bloodshed; call upon the better part of them settled in this place, and desirous of enjoying the blessings of this government, to exert themselves to the utmost, in aid of the Magistracy and Police Officers, in order to put down these offences and disorders amongst their countrymen, and to assist in discovering and bringing the offenders to justice. Several of the desperate outrages in which these people have engaged, have originated in the pernicious practise of gambling, most prevalent among them; which, both at common law, and several ancient statutes, … is an offence against the public morals, indictable when practiced for the purpose of lucre and making a livelihood of it, and in such a manner as to become a common nuisance. And what can be plainer nuisance to any neighborhood than to collect for the purpose of gambling, either in the public streets or places, or in houses of common resorts, the idle and dissolute; - to draw in unwary youth to sudden ruin, and thereby tempt them to supply their losses, by thieving, besides the consequent neglect of their lawful occupations? and this, for the purpose of lucre to some crafty gamester or a secret combination of such. The evil example to the public is obvious; the danger and nuisance to families in the immediate neighborhood is too often practically felt; and the waste of the fortune and character of the youths, who are drawn off from their ordinary and lawful occupations to this wasteful and demoralizing practice, almost inevitably follows.

...

In proportion to the increase of population and wealth in a great metropolis, it must be expected that crimes will also increase: and these can only be kept down within a moderate amount, by preventive measures in aid of the terrors of the law against flagrant transgressors. Amongst preventive means none are more efficacious than an improved and more extensive system of education; a stricter religious and moral domestic discipline in families; - the public co-operation of Gentlemen of high character and extensive influence in Society, to improve the domestic condition and comforts, and thereby to raise the character of the industrious classes of the people. The two former of those means, must in their nature, be left to be supplied principally by individual effort; but the latter can only be effected by individual and public cooperation, to which therefore, my present observations will be confined.

...

In most, if not all of the great Cities of Europe, it has been found necessary to regulate by public ordinances, those classes of laborers, who profess to serve the public at large, or to ply in the streets or on the rivers for casual employment; - such as public Porters, or Coolies, Tickah Bearers, Hackey Drivers, Boatmen, and the like. Persons of these descriptions afford whether knowingly or unknowingly, great assistance to the commission of thefts and without the help of a known public badge, it is seldom possible to discover the individuals concerned in the removal of property stolen, so as to enable the owner to have it; much more to detect their participation in the fact. Regulations of this nature seem to be peculiarly called for by the actual condition of this vast city, open as it is on all sides, containing in the mass of its population, several distinct races, - escorted to by strangers from every part of India and of the world, and like all other great crowds, peculiarly attractive to the secret thief and dexterous robber of these regions.

Facsimile: A center for early print and society.

9 ON OPIUM AND SALT TRADE

SUPPLEMENT TO
THE CALCUTTA GAZETTE,

Thursday, February 6, 1800.

Notice is hereby given,

That on Monday the 17th of next Month, at the hour of Ten o'clock in the forenoon, will be Sold by Public Auction at this Office, the whole of the remaining quantity of the Agency OPIUM, provided in the year 1798-9, viz.

        BEHAR - Chests 1,675

        BENARAS – *ditto* 379

        Total Chests 2,954

Also, about Fifty Maunds of confined OPIUM from Behar, the particulars of which will be made known at the time of Sale.

CONDITION OF SALE:

The Opium to be sold by the Chest, in Lots of five Chests each, one Rupee to be paid down to bind the bargain, and a deposit of ten per Cent on the price of each Lot, in money or public Securities, to be made by the Purchasers before the expiration of five days. In default thereof the Lot or Lots to be Resold, and all losses and expenses attending such resale, to be paid by the first Purchasers, and any profit arising thereupon to belong to Government.

The Opium to be paid for and cleared and within Two Months from the day of sale, and in case any Opium shall not be paid for and cleared out, the abovementioned deposit of Ten per Cent, and the earnest Money are to be liable to forfeiture, and the Opium will be advertised for a Ready Money Sale; all losses and expenses attending such sale to be borne by the first Purchasers, and any profit accruing from it to belong to Government.

The Public are hereby informed that no other export of Opium, besides the one hundred Chests for Europe, as stated in the first Advertisement, will be made on Account of the Honourable Company this Season.

The Public are also hereby informed, that in the providing of the Investment of Opium for the current year, the same precautions have been taken, as those observed in the preceding year, to have the drug procured and sent down in a pure state, to have only the prescribed quantity of leaves used in forming the cakes, and to have the due proportion of Opium put into each cake.

For the information of the Merchants, the following papers may be seen at this Office, at any time between the hours of ten and three O'clock previous to the day of sale.

No. 1. Instructions to the Agents in respect to the provision of the Opium.

2. Warrantees of the Agent's relative to the Opium now advertised for sale.

3. Reports of the examination of the Opium.

4. Accounts of the weight of the Opium when packed.

5. Statements of the average weight in Calcutta of six chests of each dispatch.

On the day of Sale, the abovementioned documents will be laid on the table, and samples of the Opium to be sold will be exhibited for the inspection of the Merchants, twenty two Chests of Opium, which have been reserved from the provision of Last Year, will be also shown to them, to enable them to judge of the state of preservation in which the Drugs are kept.

Published by Order of the

Board of Trade,

JOHN COTTON, See O.D.

Calcutta, Opium Office,

January 31, 1800.

Selections from the early newspapers in colonial India.

CALCUTTA GAZETTE EXTRAORDINAIRY.

FRIDAY, OCTOBER 5, 1787.

NOTICE IS HEREBY GIVEN

THAT on THIS DAY the 11th OCTOBER, with be put to SALE at the Controller's Office at Calcutta, 1,68,000 Maunds of

BULWA AND CHITTAGONG SALT

The Produce of 1193. B.S. being the part of the quantity sold on the 7th September last, but for which the purchasers have failed to make their deposits, agreeably to the terms of the advertisements of the 27th August.

The SALT will be exposed to sale at specific prices, including the Rowannah duty of thirty sicca rupees per 100 maunds.

Printed tickets, specifying the quantity and places at which the Salt is to be delivered, under the signature of the Comptroller, will be given for the delivery of each lot.

The lots will be fixed at 3000 mds. each at an even seale of 82 S Wt.

The Salt is to be transported from the places of delivery at the risk of the purchasers. One rupee to be paid down on each lot to bind the bargain.

ACCOUNT of the Quantity of SALT to be SOLD by PUBLIC AUCTION.

33,000		186	00-Jan	4 Months.
30,000		186	0.75	do.
12,000		190	0.75	do.
66,000		186		do.
	1,41,000	2,62,740	0.75	
24,000		172	0.75	do.
3,000		176		do.
	27,000	46,560		
Maunds	1,68,000 S. Rups.	3,09,300		

The Deposit to be made in Company's Paper, to be received at Par, for the principal, within five Days after the Sale.

One half of the Amount deposited will be returned to the Purchaser, on his clearing out one half of the Salt purchased by him; the balance to remain in deposit, until the Clearance of the whole shall be made.

The Salt not cleared out by the date specified for that purpose, shall be resold on account of the first Purchaser, and any deficiency falling therein shall be made good from his deposit.

Every Clearance to be made in ready money, reserving the deposit to the last.

No Clearance shall be made for a less quantity than five hundred Maunds.

All Clearance to be paid directly into the Controller's Office, who will thereupon issue the orders for delivery with the Rowannahs.

OFFICE, the 4th October, 178.7.
THOMAS CALVERT, Compt

10 ON SLAVES AND ABOLITION

CALCUTTA GAZETTE EXTRAORDINARY

Monday, July 27, 1789.

PROCLMATION

Whereas information, the truth of which cannot be doubted, has been received by the GOVERNOR GENERAL in COUNCIL that many NATIVES and some EUROPEANS, in opposition to the Laws and Ordinance of this Country and the dictates of Humanity, have been for a long time in the practice of Purchasing or Collecting Natives of both Sexes, Children as well as Adult, for the purpose pf exporting them for Sale as SLAVES in different parts of India or elsewhere, and WHEREAS the GOVERNOR GENERAL in COUNCIL is determined to exert to the utmost extent the Power and Authority vested in him, in order to prevent such practise in future, and to deter by the most exemplary punishment those Persons who are not to be otherwise restrained from committing the offence. His LORDSHIP hereby DECLARES that all and every

Person or Persons, subject to the Jurisdiction of the Supreme Court, or in any respect to the Authority of this Government, who shall in future be concerned directly or indirectly in the above-mentioned inhuman and detestable Traffic, shall be Prosecuted with the utmost rigour in the Supreme Court at the expense of the Company, and, if British born Subjects, shall be forthwith ordered to Europe, or if such Person or Persons be not Subject to the Court's jurisdiction he or they, upon information being given to the Magistrate of the Place or District in which the offence shall have been committed, shall be apprehended by him, and kept in confinement, to be dealt with according to the Laws of the Country.

And thus no one may plead ignorance hereof, the SUPERINTENDANTS of the Police of the Town of Calcutta, and the MAGISTRATES of ADAWLUTS in the several parts of the Country are hereby required to give immediate Notice of this Proclamation in such manner as shall render the knowledge of it universal to Persons of all Descriptions, and to repeat the Same on the First Day of January in every Year: They are further directed to pay the strictest attention to the Regulations contained in it, and to take the most active steps in their power to enforce them.

And that all Persons offending against this proclamation may be brought to punishment for the same, and the unhappy Sufferers rescued from misery, a Reward of One Hundred Sicca Rupees is hereby offered for the discovery of every such offender to be paid on his conviction before the Supreme Court of Judicature, or before the Magistrate of the District, and of Fifty Rupees for every Person of either Sex, who shall be delivered from Slavery or illegal confinement in consequence of such discovery. The Money shall be paid to the Informer or Informers and for their application to the Secretary of Government and presenting to him a Certificate …

The GOVERNOR GENERAL in COUNCIL further recommends to British Commercial Houses and Private Individuals, to insist as far as depends upon them, in carrying these Regulations into effect by taking the most effectual means in their power to disassuade the Commander of their Ships or Vessels, or of Ships or Vessels configured to them, or other wise placed under their directions from carrying out … this Order to sell them for SLAVES.

The MASTER ATTENDANT of this Port is hereby forbidden to grant in future [permission to the] Commander of which shall not have previously declared upon Oath that there are not then on board, …any Native to be exported as SLAVES with an intent to dispose of them …

And the MASTER ATTENDANT is hereby directed to give Notice to all the Native Pilots that is any should Pilot out any Vessel having on board Natives of this Description, knowing or believing them to be such, the Privilege of Piloting will be taken from them for ever, and their Names and Offences registered. And that no one may plead ignorance of this order, it is hereby directed that it be placed constantly in view at the Banksaul in the English and Country Languages.

PROCLAIMED at FORT WILLIAM in BENGAL, this 22nd day of July, 1789.

By Order of the GOVERNOR GENERAL in COUNCIL,

E. HAY, Secretary to the Government.

Facsimile: A center for early print and society.

[ON ABOLITION]

Newspaper: Not known; Calcutta Feb. 21, 1788.

We are happy to observe, from the speech of the Prince Regent, that our Court continues its endeavors to effect the entire abandonment of the slave trade. We anxiously wait for the conventions it has recently concluded with Spain and Portugal, with a view to that object, observing in the interim that, from the terms in which they are mentioned, the friends of humanity need not be greatly disappointed if they do not prove all they could wish.

The cause of Abolition has had to encounter the most formidable difficulties in every step of its progress; and the success it has already experienced, notwithstanding the open or secret resistance of enemies, and the lukewarm support of many who were or pretended to be its friends, should afford encouragement to the supporters of every good design to adhere to it with an honest pertinacity.

The slave trade has been abolished by law, as far as regards the British dominions and British subjects, an object which was not secured without a struggle of twenty years with ignorance, prejudice, and self-interest. If the ardour and perseverance of the abolitionists continue unabated, the present generation will witness the entire extermination of the odious traffic in human beings torn from their native land.

Our attention has ben particularly directed to this subject by an article which has been reprinted from the English newspapers in most of the Calcutta papers, including our own. We allude to the highly important case of the Louis, a French Slave-trader captured off Cape Mesurada, on the windward coast of African by a British cruiser, and condemned in the Vice Admiralty Court of Sierra Leone. …

The necessary consequences of the abolition laws of Britain and other nations have been an enhancement of the price Slaves of America and a diminution in Africa, which together render the trade very profitable to those who continue it. The laws of some countries will permit it, with or without restrictions; and the interlopers of all nations strive to elude the prohibitive regulations of their various governments. The vast extent of these coasts where slaves are obtainable, and other circumstances, give great facilities to this clandestine trade, the total extermination of which is urged by every consideration of policy and humanity.

If the principles of natural and international law laid down by Sir Walter Scott are destined to be adopted by our courts, and to govern their decisions, we fear the most formidable obstacles will oppose themselves to that extermination. Let us take the most favourable suppositions. Let us suppose all the governments of the world to foresee and confess the barbarity of the Slave-trade; and in conformity to treaties concluded among themselves to forbid under the most severe penalties, its prosecution by their subjects – these prohibitions would be illusory or ineffectual, unless every single state professed both, the means and sincere desire of enforcing them. Sir W. Scott's view of the subject does not permit the most powerful and best intentioned in their number to enforce the inhibitions promulgated by all.

Should this interpretation of the law of nations become current and of authority, the new and most formidable impediment it creates in the way of the total eradication of the Slave-trade, which can be overcome only by a series of conventions to be concluded with all the different maritime trade. It will be necessary to stipulate that, if any two or more states forbid the slave trade to their subjects, the courts of all shall have an effectual jurisdiction in this matter over the vessels and subjects of all. If no such effectual jurisdiction be recognized, it then becomes absolutely necessary that every single Government shall maintain, on the western coast of Africa and elsewhere, a naval establishment sufficient to enforce its own prohibitory laws, an effort which some of them would be unable and other unwilling to make. This arrangement, by which the cruizers of any given state would be restricted from checking the slave dealing speculations of foreigners, if it did not practically remove all hindrance in the way of the traffic except those arising from non-importation laws in the countries where slaves now find a sale, would be at best a prodigious waste of resource and public effort.

ABOUT US.

Facsimile is an independent research center that works on early print and society in colonial India. To learn more, please visit us at: www.colonialprint.wordpress.com

Also, visit www.earlycolonialprint.org to learn more about the emergence of early print in colonial Bengal.

www.ingramcontent.com/pod-product-compliance
Lightning Source LLC
Chambersburg PA
CBHW061251040426
42444CB00010B/2342